© S.E. Burr 2018

ISBN-13:
978-1986745581

ISBN-10:
1986745589

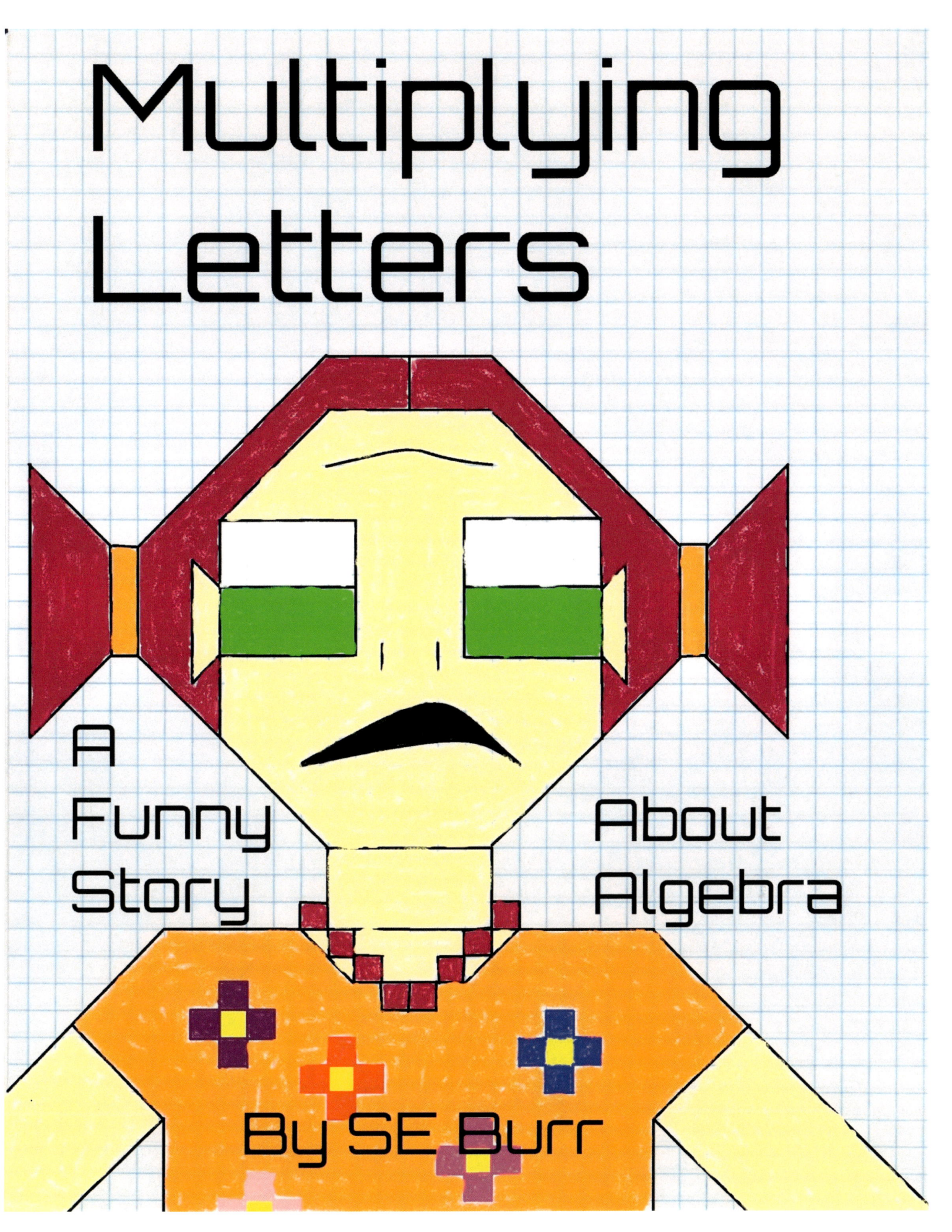

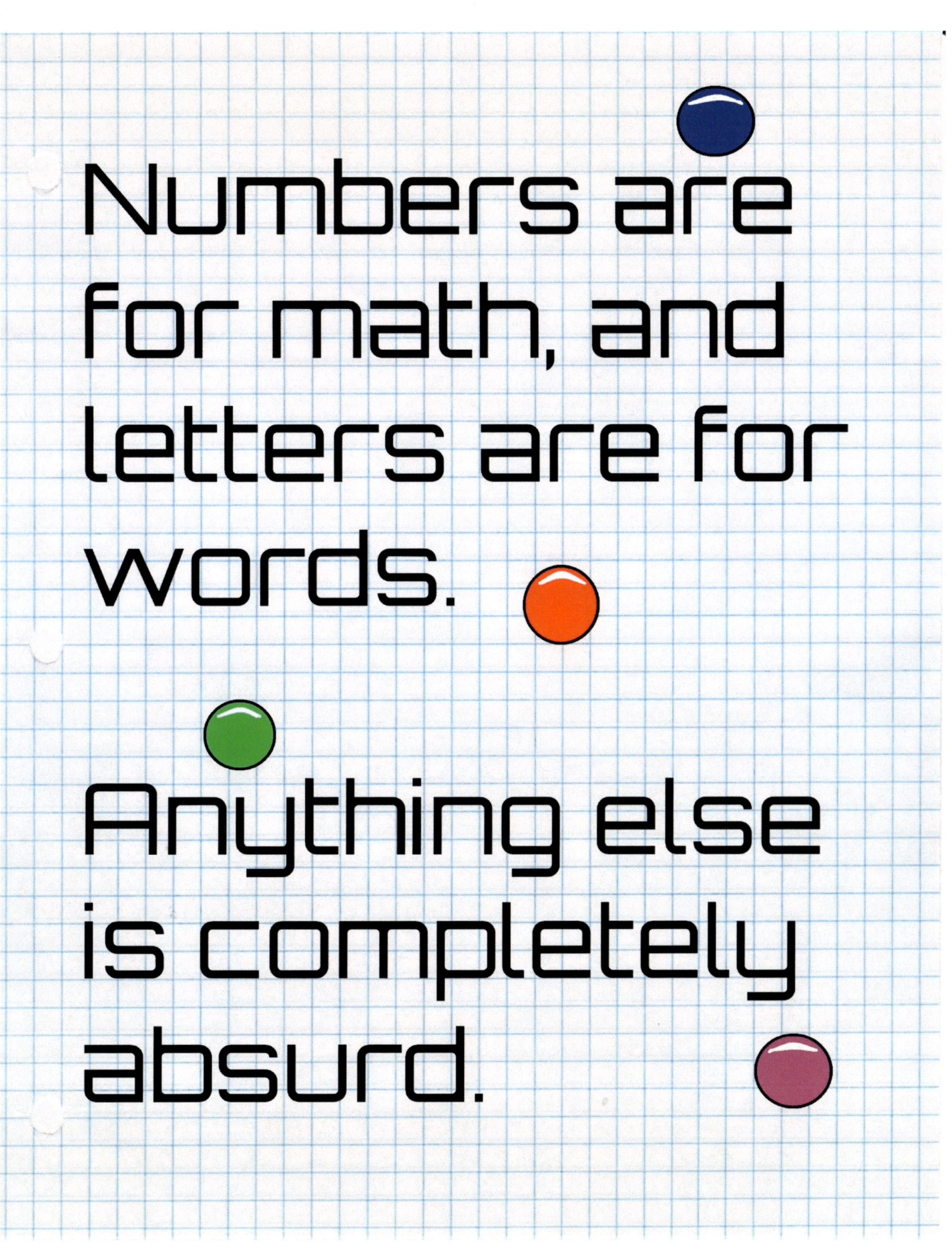

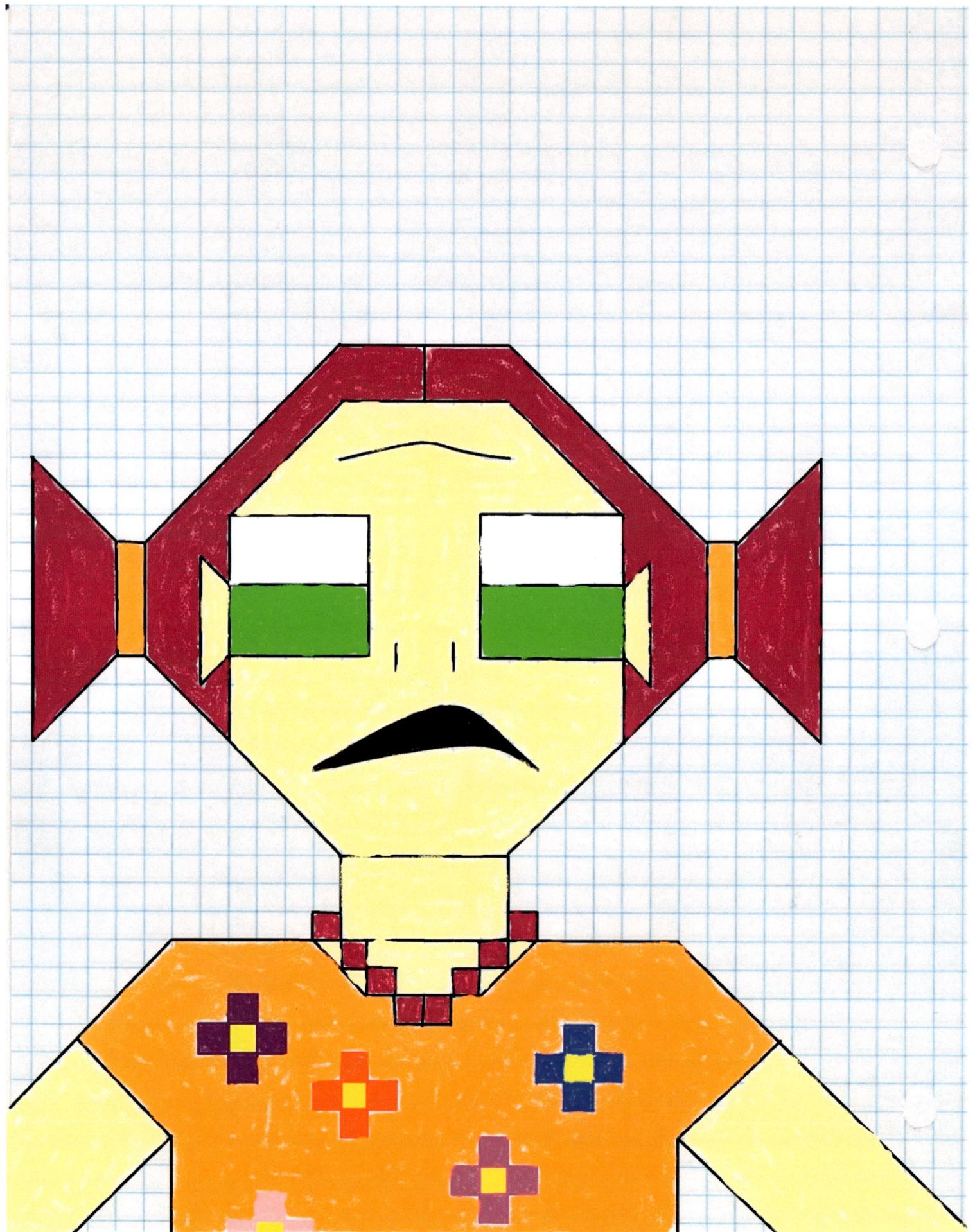

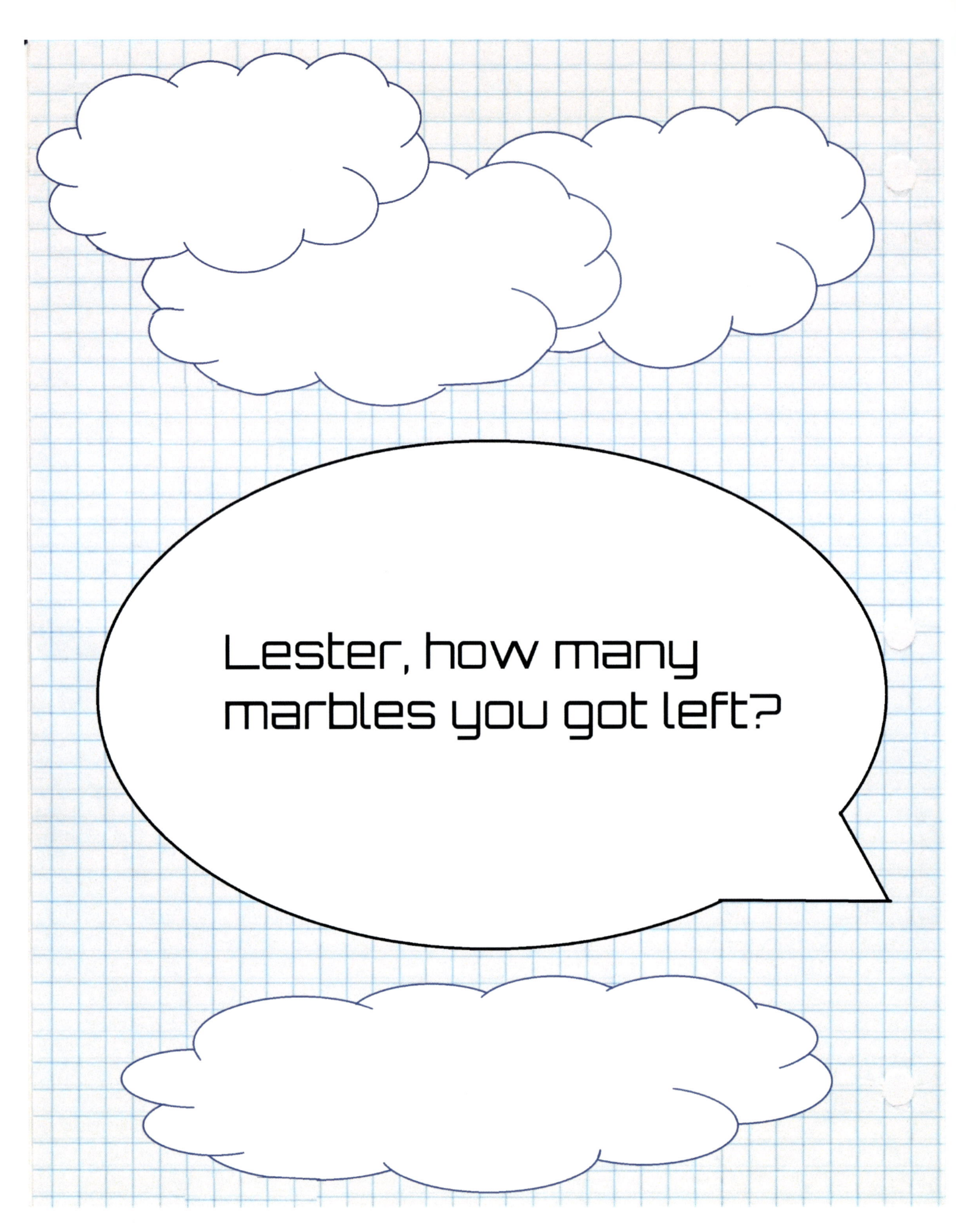

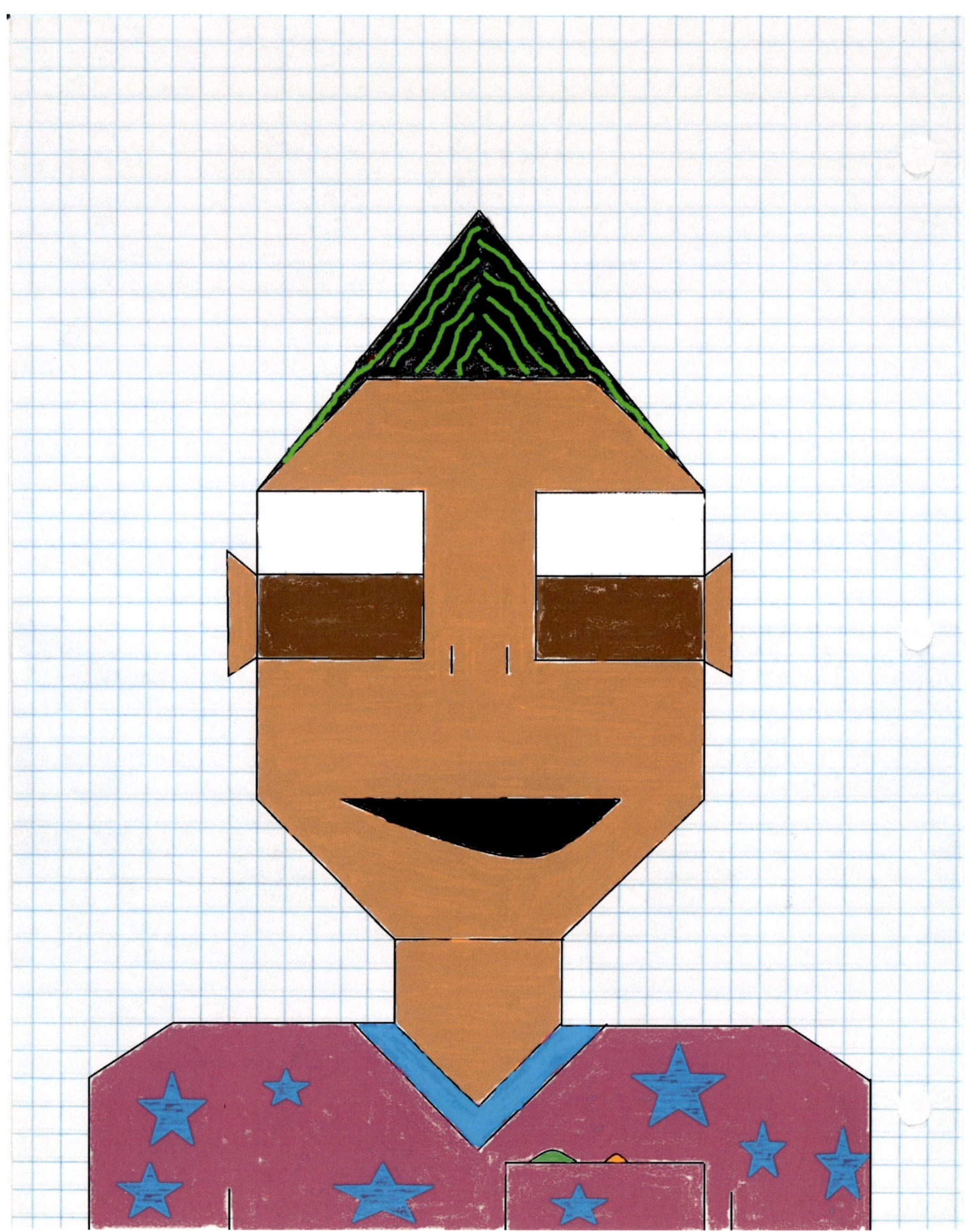

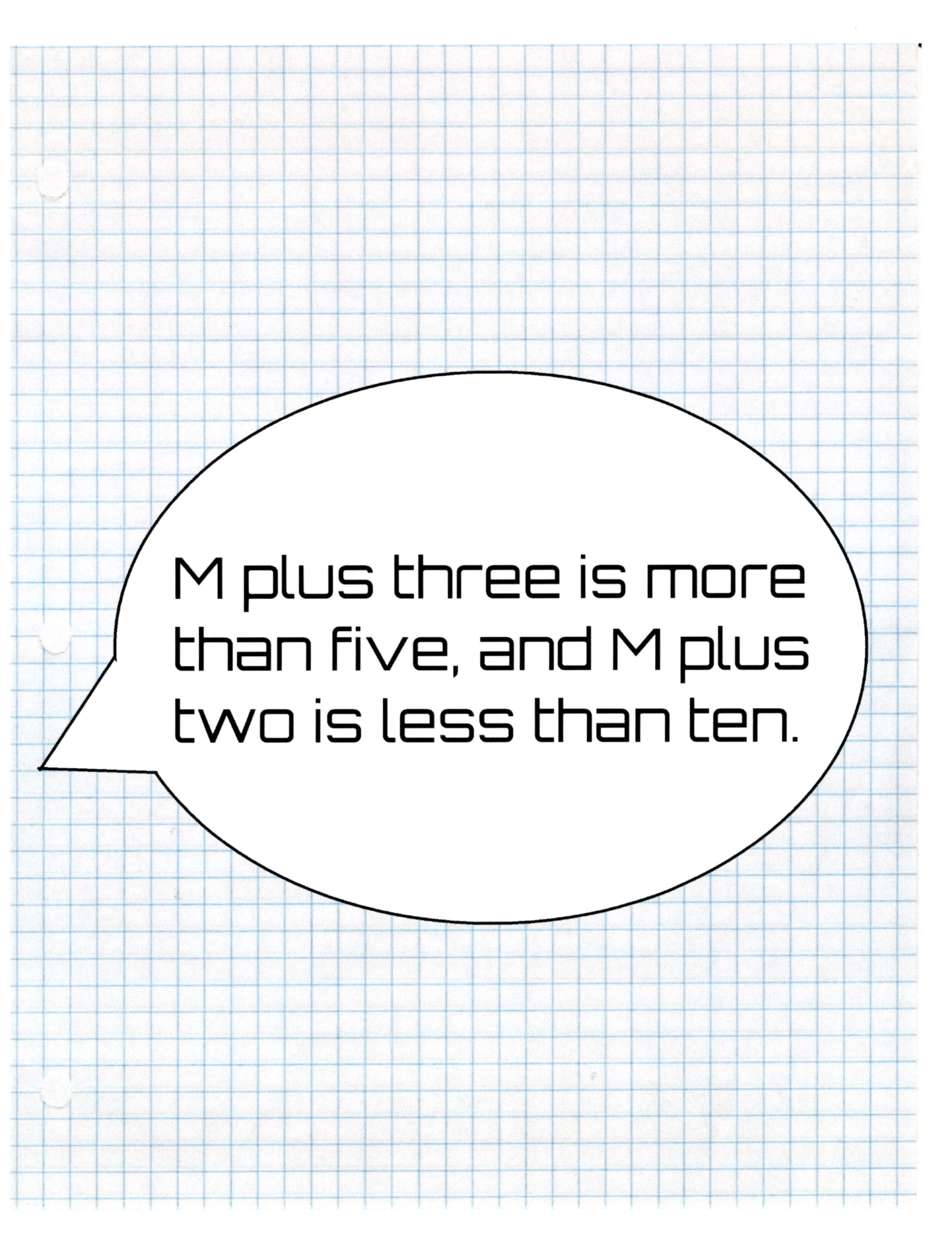

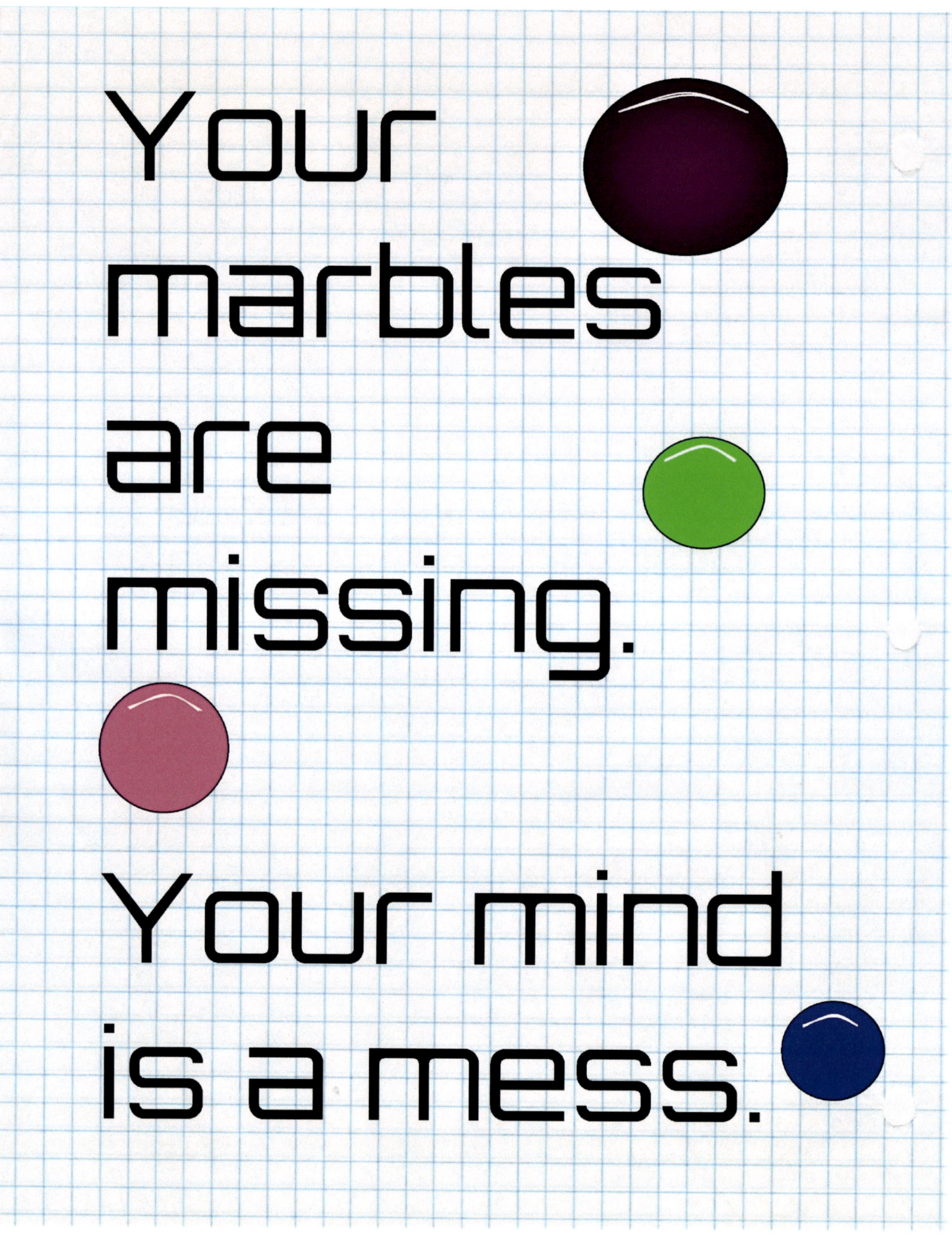

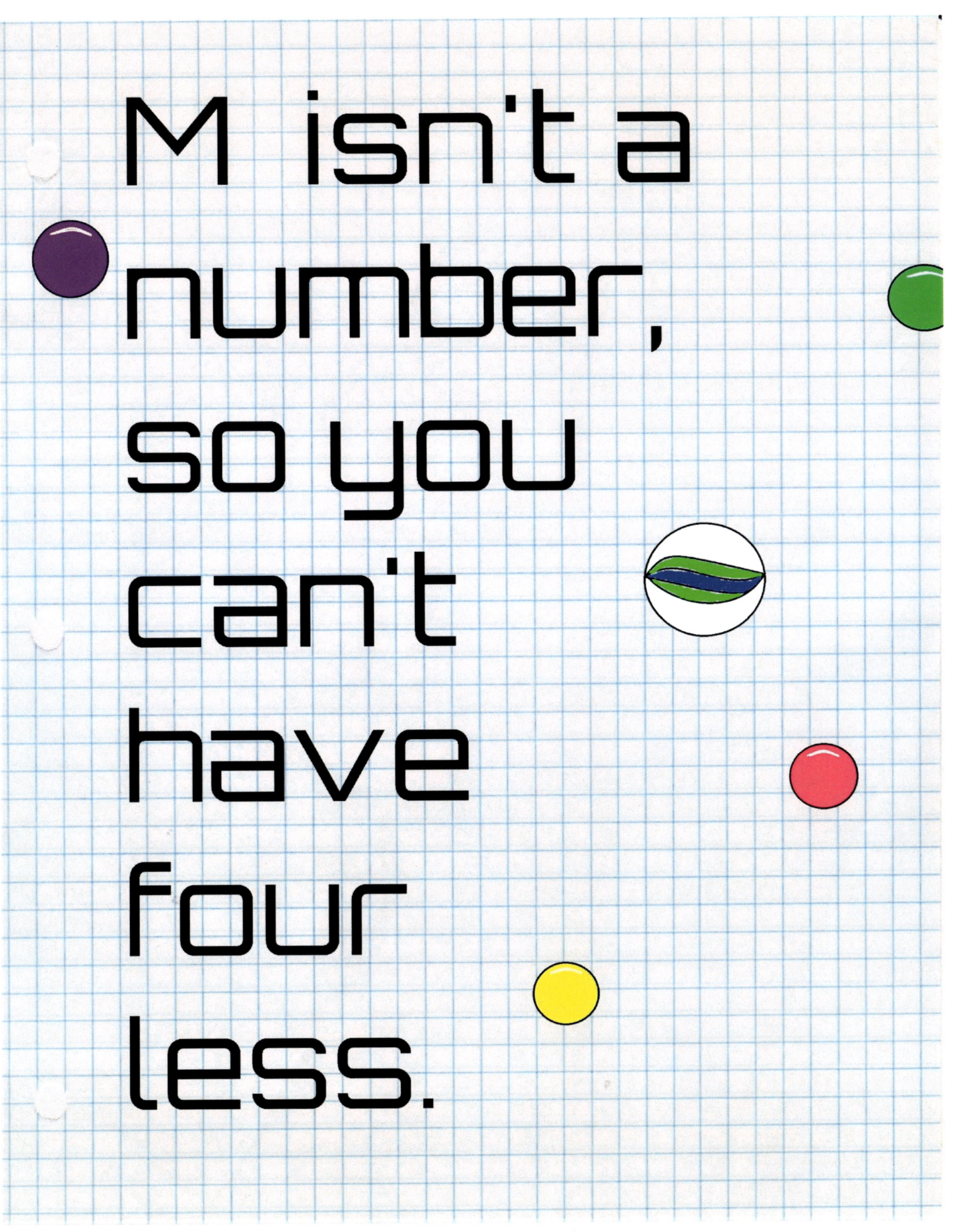

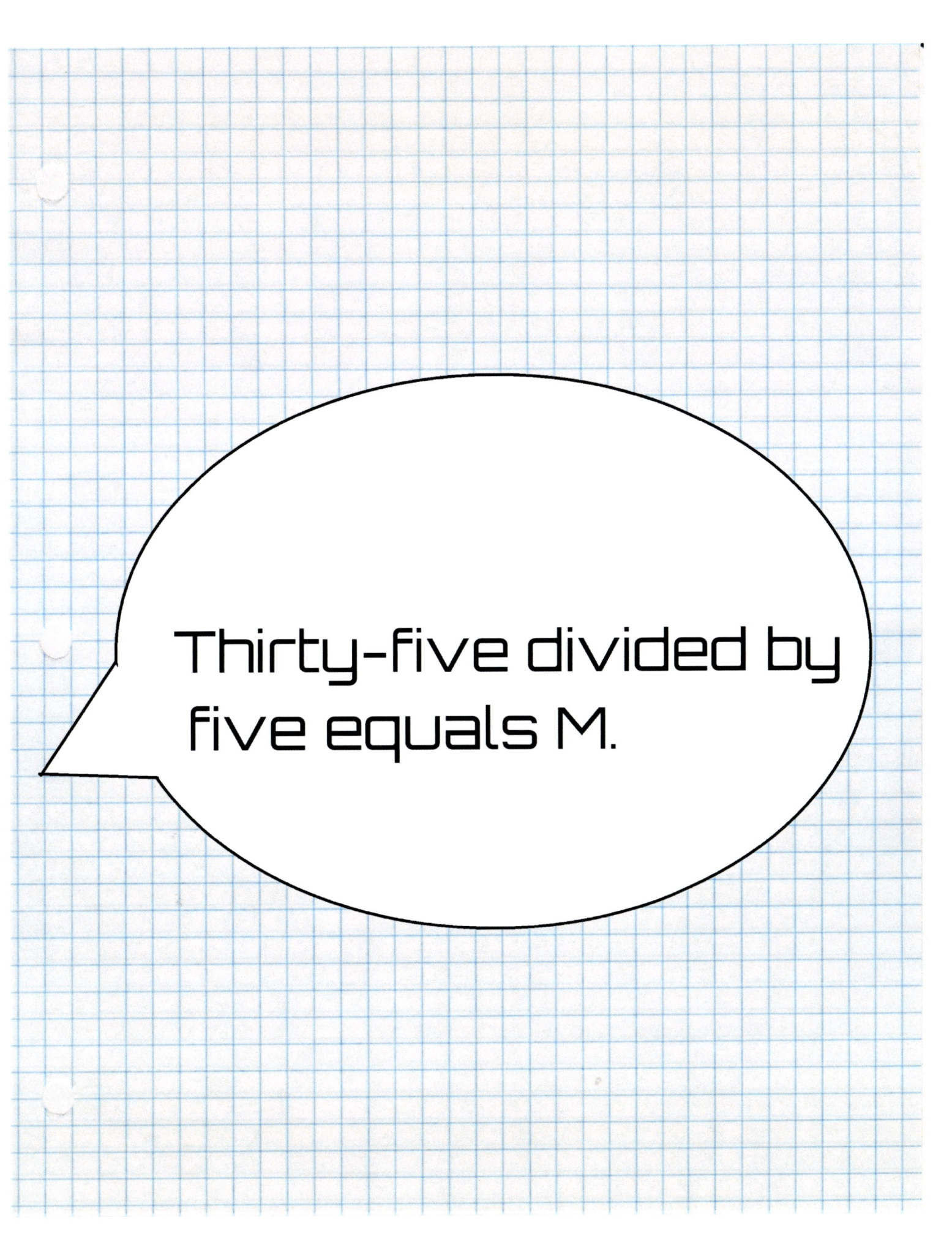

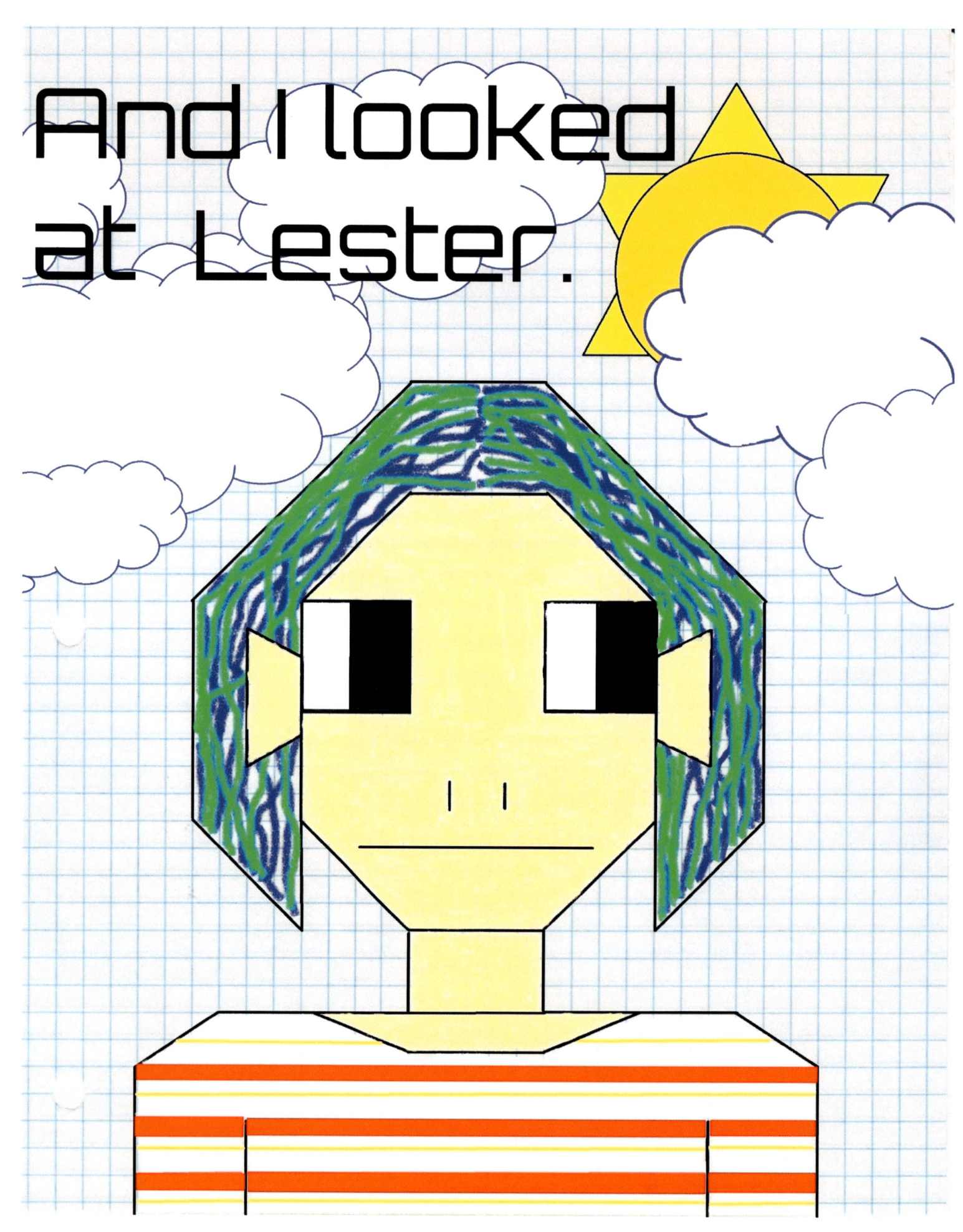

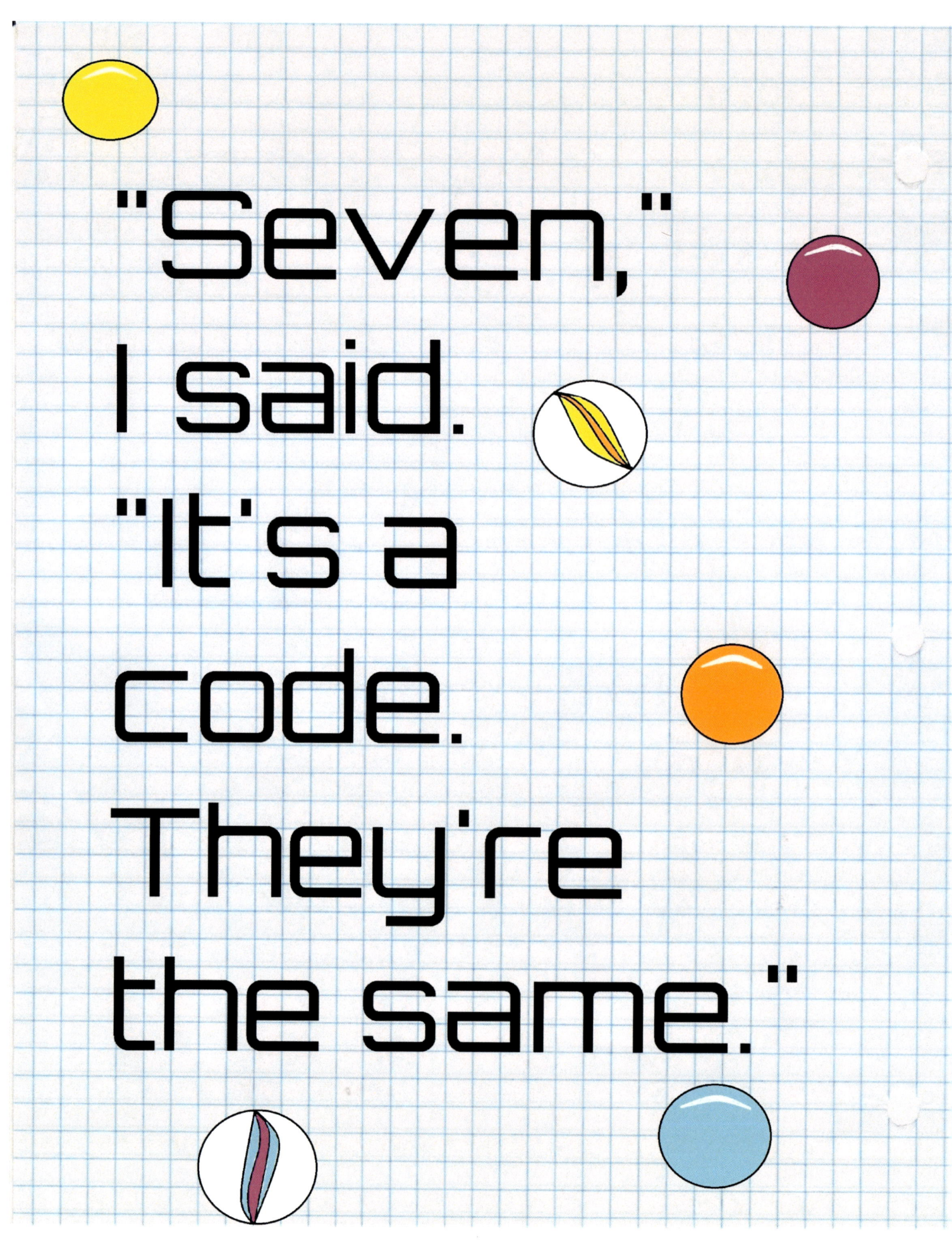

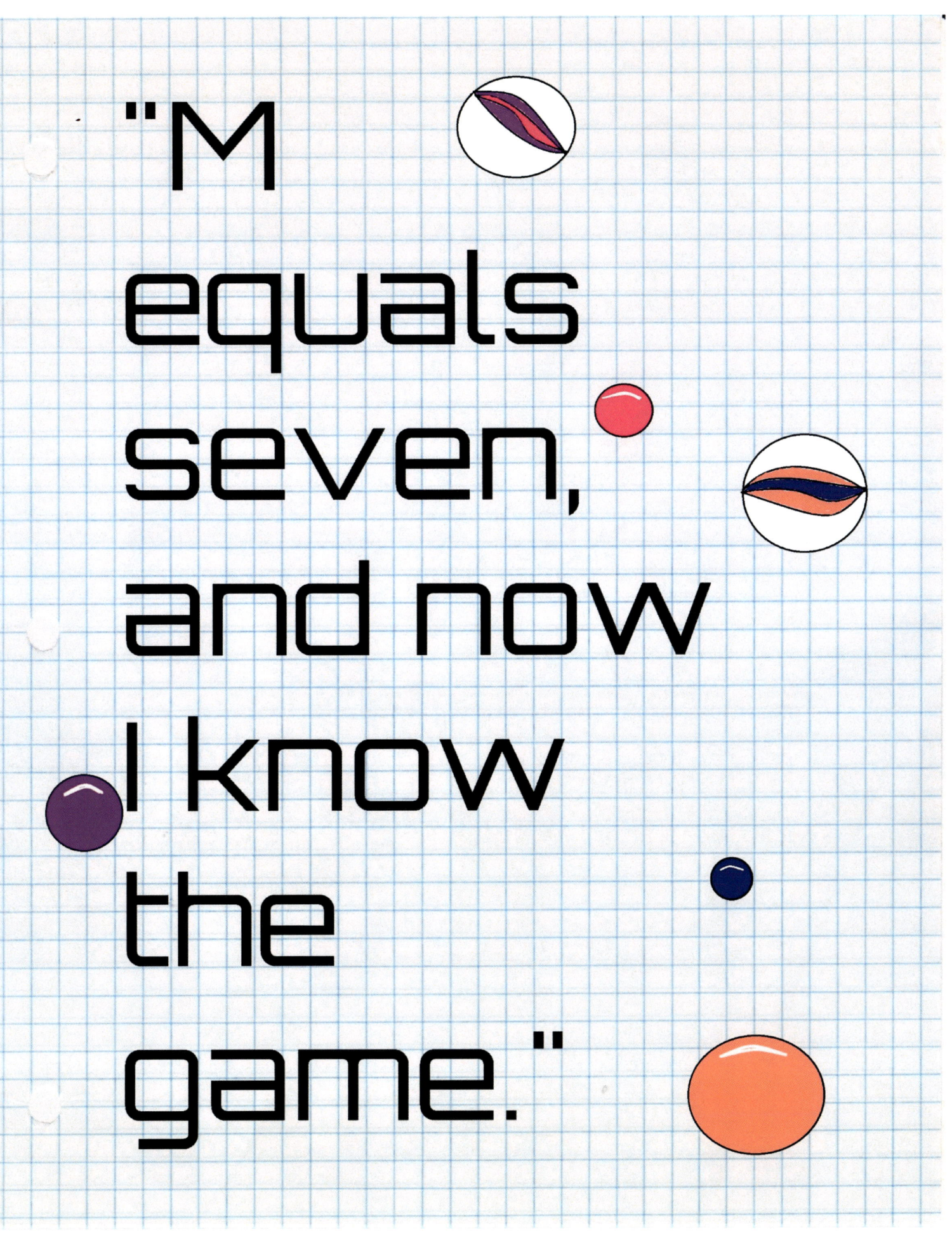

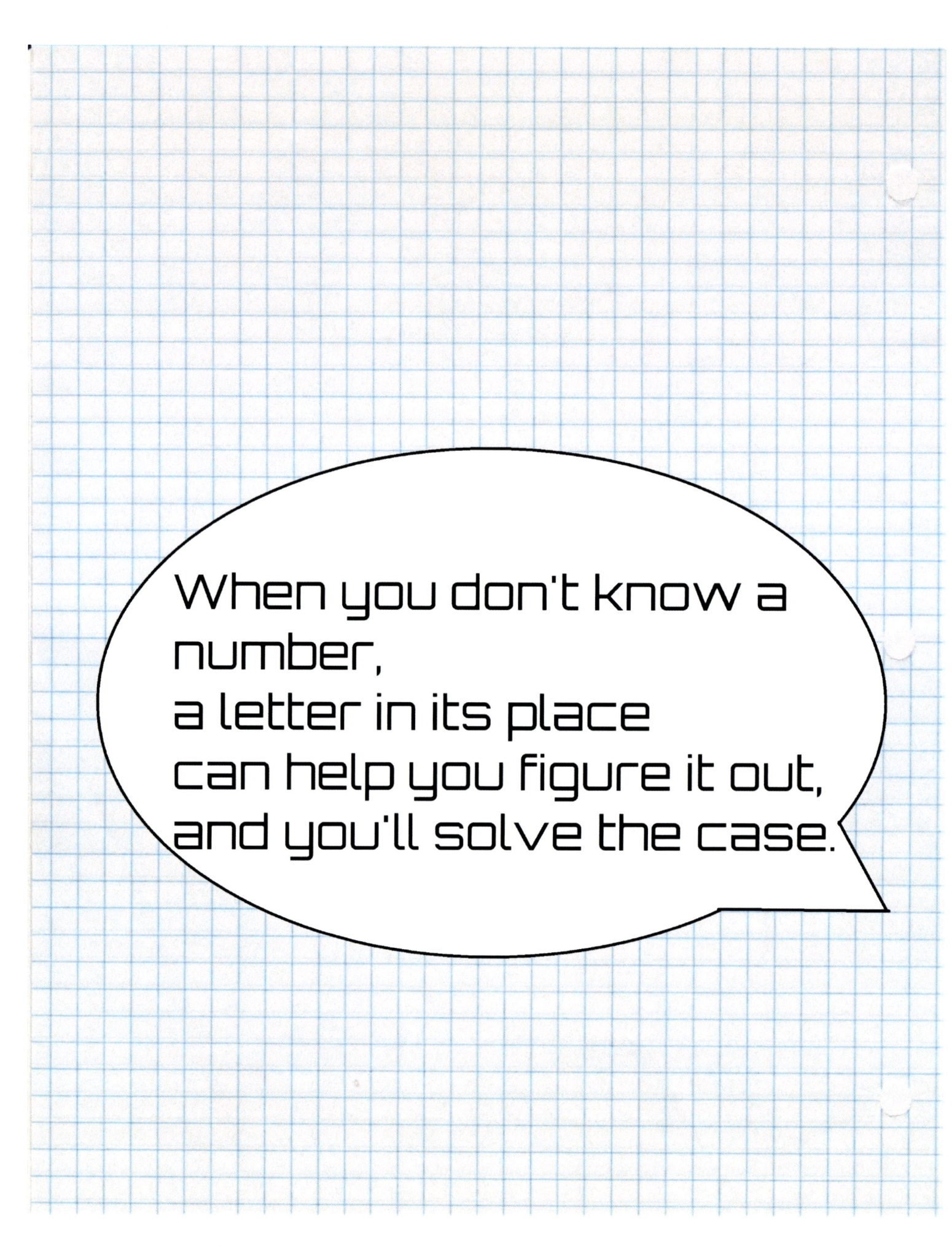

Lester, you have seven marbles. You're not a marble-less man.

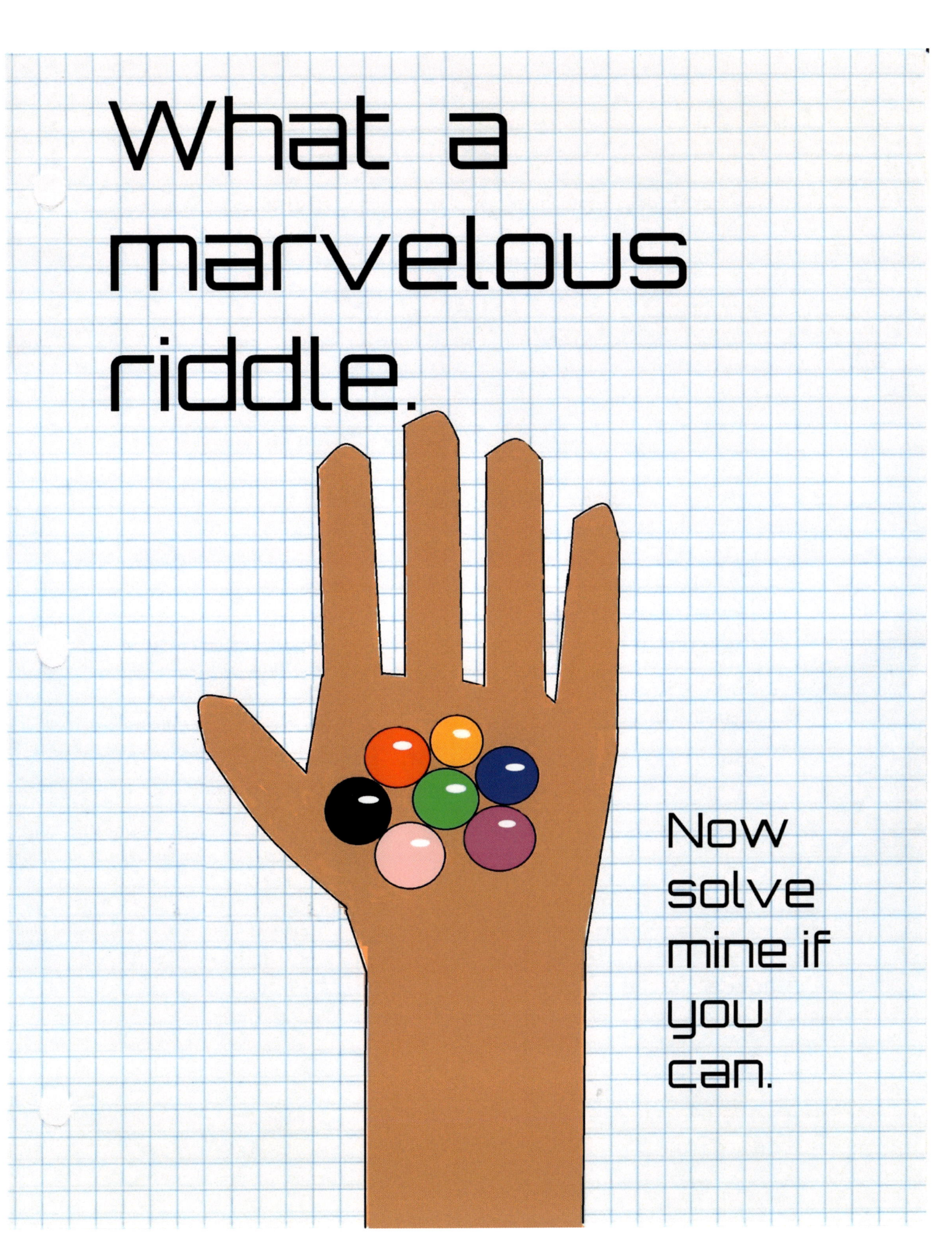

Examples:

M + 2 = 5

You may be able to figure this one out just by thinking about it.

What plus two equals five?

Three!

But sometimes they're trickier. If you need to work it out on paper, you can do it this way:

1. You need to get M by itself on one side of the equal sign.

2. To move the 2 to the other side, you can subtract 2 from both sides.

$$M + 2 = 5$$
$$ -2\ -2$$
$$M = 3$$

3. The 2's on the M side, disappear, because "M + 2 - 2" is the same as "M + 0" or just "M".

4. And now you have the answer:

M = 3

Let's do some more:

$A - 5 = 3$	$B \cdot 4 = 20$	$C \div 8 = 5$
$+5 \quad +5$	$\div 4 \quad \div 4$	$\cdot 8 \quad \cdot 8$
$A = 8$	$B = 5$	$C = 40$

(In algebra, we often use a dot to mean times.)

Okay, now you try:

$D + 3 = 7$	$E - 6 = 3$	$F \cdot 2 = 14$
$-\_\_ \quad -\_\_$		
$D = \_\_$	$E = \_\_$	$F = \_\_$
$G \div 3 = 3$	$H + 9 = 10$	$I - 16 = 4$
$G = \_\_$	$H = \_\_$	$I = \_\_$
$J \cdot 3 = 18$	$K + 12 = 23$	$L \div 10 = 3$
$J = \_\_$	$K = \_\_$	$L = \_\_$

Here are Lester's riddles and how I finally figured out how many marbles he had:

"M times two is more than eight, and M times ten is less than eighty."

$$M \cdot 2 > 8 \qquad\qquad M \cdot 10 < 80$$
$$\div 2 \;\; \div 2 \qquad\qquad \div 10 \;\; \div 10$$
$$M > 4 \qquad\qquad\qquad M < 8$$

"M plus three is more than five, and M plus two is less than ten."

$$M + 3 > 5 \qquad\qquad M + 2 < 10$$
$$-3 \;\; -3 \qquad\qquad -2 \;\; -2$$
$$M > 2 \qquad\qquad\qquad M < 8$$

I already knew this!

"M minus four is more than two, and M minus 2 is more than four."

$$M - 4 > 2 \qquad\qquad M - 2 > 4$$
$$+4 \;\; +4 \qquad\qquad +2 \;\; +2$$
$$M > 6 \qquad\qquad\qquad M > 6$$

Both of these told me the same thing!

"Thirty-five divided by five equals M."

$$35 \div 5 = M$$
$$\cdot 5 \;\; \cdot 5$$
$$7 = M$$

This answer matched everything Lester had already told me so I knew it was right!

Check out the other books in the "Funny Math Stories" series, including:

1% Clean: A Funny Story About Fractions and Percents

And

1% Messy: A Companion Workbook to 1% Clean

There are more Funny Math Stories coming soon!

S.E. Burr has other books for young people available now including the teen series, "Gobbled" and the picture book, *The Everything Puzzle*.

Made in the USA
Columbia, SC
10 April 2020